QUEER
HEARTACHE

QUEER
HEARTACHE

"Human Resources" originally published as "At the Medicaid Office" in *Troubling the Line* (Nightboat Books, June 2011). nightboat.org

"Not Girls Like You," "Sunrise" and "Sunset" originally published "Someday Soon" and "Silicone Dicks," in *Flicker and Spark* (Lowbrow Press, February 2013). lowbrowpress.com

ISBN paperback: 978-0-9851105-2-9
ISBN e-book: 978-0-9851105-3-6
LOC: 2016939098

Cover art by Jess X. Chen
Layout and book design by Simone Wolff

Contents

Getting Braces	1
Plastic	4
Bumper Stickers	8
Hello, My Gender Is...	11
Sunset	17
Sunrise	20
Not Girls Like You	23
Queer Heartache	26
Edwin's Poem	31
Josh and Drake	35
Choice	38
SHE	41
Faggots	44
Pussy Stitches	48
Human Resources	51
Speaking English	55

GETTING BRACES

When I was 12,
> My mother asked me if I wanted braces.

She asked because some of her friend's kids
> were getting them.

In school, kids were starting to have mouths full
> of neon bands
>> and obsess over brushing.

I told my mother
> *no*

because the other thing
> kids were talking about

was the cost.

See, braces back then cost over $2000,
> and I knew my mom

didn't have that kind of money.
> I knew my mom

didn't make that kind of money in a month.

So now I have crooked teeth,
> and I floss
>> A LOT
>>> breaking the string between the molars.

When you have crooked teeth,
> you use a lot of floss.

And even if we couldn't afford braces,
> we could steal floss

from the poor people's dentist—
> unless someone else took it all first.

My senior year, I had the worst yearbook quote ever:

Affluent is forever

I wanted to be rich,
        filthy rich,
                to buy things,
          to want things,
                to have what other kids had.

It's the sting of poverty that inspired me,
        feeling bone-hungry on weekends,
watching my mother find dinner
        in dirty Chinatown trash cans,
being ashamed of getting government lunches.

Picking up my blue ticket instead of green
        in front of all the kids,
walking to school in the dark cold,
        using memory to navigate,
stealing quarters from my mother's purse,
        catching pigeons for food outside the zoo,
getting shoo'd by the cops.

We were poor and desperate
        and all we thought about was money.
Obsessed with money:
        how much we had,
how to get more,
        how to get more to give
to our family,
        our friends,
                our neighbors
                        who had just as little as us.

We are not made to swim upstream through poverty.
        The lines at social services are so long,
the medical care punching us in the jaw,

        the translations saying the wrong thing,
making us come back a tenth time.

These agencies are not for us.
        They are meant to hold us in place,
keep us tired, and hungry, and forgotten,

        when our names cannot even be written
in our tongues.

So I never got braces.

Instead I learned how the systems
        were working against us,
so that everyone could stay alive another day,
        find another way to make a buck stretch.

And I ain't ashamed of these hardships,
        'cause I know at the end of the day,
someone will tell me how to lie

        to get a new social security card,
how to fudge the papers for another family member,
        how to share and celebrate and tell the stories
of the generations.

        And you don't need straight teeth to talk story.

I know that even if your chops are jagged,
        you can still smile,
                bright as your mouth can open.

Plastic

Paper. . .or plastic?

Some choose paper
        so that they can recycle it,
                help the environment
                        and humankind.
Some choose plastic
        because they don't have the time
                to deal with the bag breaking.

But my people choose plastic because...
                a plastic bag is the fabric of our community!

When I was a kid,
        I remember the Spidermen and Wonder Women
                flying high on top shiny new lunch bags—
                        polyester and vinyl—
                overstuffed with good kine lunches, like:
        musubi with furikake, chicken legs, adobo,
soda frozen until ice.

But—my maddah packs white rice
        with a little bit of pork and cabbage,
                puts dat sucka in a plastic bag
                        and gives me one old bottle
                                filled with wata.
After that, dat bugga
        holds my books, my shoes, my clothes.

It's gonna pick up Keri's grandpa's pickled mangoes,
        anything that can fit inside a plastic bag,
                and as long as it's intact,
        you better bring it back
'cause we go use um until it's got pukas.

And my maddah keeps da plastic
        on da face of da cell phone screen,
                until the numbers can't be seen because dirt
        has formed a thin layer, clouding up the entire face,

and da remote control is wrapped so thick in plastic wrap,
        you could use it to play basketball!

And my couch speaks to me in a squeak,
        because separating my ass from the seat
                is twenty layers of saran wrap protecting it
                        from leaks, and spills, and stains
        for centuries to come!

My TV, my digital cameras, my laptop,
        everything wrapped in a plastic-wrap condom!
        Nothing goes out, nothing gets in.

When I was a kid,
        I didn't have a recycling bin,
          'cause in my house,
                when you buy one yogurt,
                      you don't just get a yogurt.

You get a yogurt and a potted plant,
        you get a yogurt and a mug,
                you get a yogurt and a Barbie doll bathtub.

So no waste, grandma says,
        'causes you can always use one thing for another.

Like dat plastic peanut butter jar:
        when the creaminess is gone,
          dat jar will live on

to contain a serving of mom's nasty-ass soup
            for you to take home and drink
whether you like it or not.

Dat jar will house herbal remedies,
            peanuts, pennies, paper clips,
                        it'll go to the restaurant after that to collect tips,
            then hold cornstarch, sugar, honey, and more.

I remember opening the refrigerator door
            being a confusing experience each time, 'cause
                        I open a pudding container
                                    only to find leftover stir fry,
                        a cookie tin filled with eggs dyed brown.

I found shredded cabbage in a Lay's bag!

And now when I look back,
            I find it a little bit funny,
                        but we reused because we didn't have money.

We weren't rebelling against the economy
            for the sake of making waves—
                        my grandparents saved pennies
                                    like chunks of gold,
                        wrapped everything in plastic wrap,
            reused plastic bags, jars, take out utensils, tofu tubs,
any sort of packaging that could have another life.

So that they could give us another life.

They sacrificed, and scraped, and saved,
            so that I could grow up and make waves
                        that carry their stories in the fabric of my lines.

So now, I keep a barrel of plastic bags under my sink,
and I drink water from old jelly jars,
store little candy bars in tofu tubs,

while keeping life and love
inside a plastic bag
I carry in my heart.

Bumper Stickers

When I was 19,

I bought a second-hand, rusty old Forest Green 1997 Jeep.

I had just moved to Boston from Hawaii, and I learned what snow was.

So I bought a large vehicle to drive through blizzards.

The next thing I did was cover that old thing in stickers.

I finally owned something I could customize, express myself on.

So I covered it with squiggly rainbows, curvy rainbows, equal signs,

and when I ran out of space, I bumper-stickered the sides,

adding a couple of the *forest is within, respect farmers*, peace symbols,

and whatever other liberal expression was available.

I loved that car.

It said everything I wanted to say

before I even knew what all of that meant!

I spent all my extra money on stickers that year.

On a quiet night after coming home from a slam,

I parked my car and went home to study.

Later, when I needed a Dunkin' Donuts run,

I returned to my vehicle to find that all my lights were smashed,

the mirrors broken off,

the tires kicked and peed on.

Mine had been the only car in the parking lot vandalized,

and I was the most dyed-hair freaky-looking queer

on our conservative campus.

The police told me it might be a hate crime,

but they didn't have evidence or time to support it.

They never found out who did it.

They didn't try very hard.

See, hate crimes give authorities a fire escape,

so to fan the flame they assigned me my own body guard,

a police car that followed me

every single time I went on or off campus.

Their profiling was supposed to protect me.

That year, for my own safety, an administrator told me

I should take the bumper stickers off my newly fixed car.

Later, they assigned me to the farthest dorm on campus.

Hiding my body.

I didn't have the words at that time to explain

that every time I drove down the street and saw a rainbow,

I felt seen.

That person may never know me,

but a little sticker gave me hope

that one day I'd find my communities,

communities that say:

come as you're changing,

come as you are,

just come because we'll have a place for you.

A plate of food, a spot, a glass,

and we will love you because you're home.

Hello, My Gender Is...

They say that gender should be as simple
as gay or straight.

They say if you are attracted to the opposite gender,
you're straight.

They say if you are attracted to the same gender,
you're gay.

Therefore, if you have a penis, you're a man.
And if you have a vagina, you're a woman.

Straight shot, straight answer. Gender.

See gender is:
man next to woman, not touching, but separate.

Gender is:
America's controlled nationalism bullshit.

Gender is:
birth certificates for babies born into gender,

housing applications, check boxes,
and even getting email addresses: this is gender.

But I ask you,
is it truly worth the embarassment?

Imprisonment? Or harassment?
For your gender identity?

So excuse me, they say,
are you a man or woman?

And you like a boy now,
so do you wanna be straight?

And you've changed your name to Kit now,
so you're straight—right?

But back when you were Laura,
you were gay?

As if sexuality and gender were something
that you could purchase on impulse,

pulling up to the register and carefully picking out
gay, straight, man, or woman,

neatly packaged for easy consumption.
Then you should be able to do it with ease.

Purchasing a gold-foiled bar of gay,
and plastic bag of man,

and walking out of the grocery store,
fabulously onto the set of *Queer Eye*.

But it's not that easy.

Because sometimes my gender is...
boy who looks like a girl, who likes boys.

And sometimes my gender is...
trans,

and sometimes my gender is...
chillin' out in between.

But most of the time, my gender is...
fuck you mind your own business!

Because gender is so rigidly defined,
neatly outlined and nicely colonized,

organized, and clearly understandable.
Unchangeable.

Yet the gap is becoming gendered,
and I'm standing in line for the restroom with

girls, birls, boys, bis, transsexual, transgender,
queer, questioning, curious, polyamorous, intersex,

flexual, asexual, trisexual, omnisexual, multisexual,
pansexual, gender neutral, genderqueer, genderfluid,

multigendered, polygendered, androgynous, drag king,
drag queen, heteroflexible, butch, femme, fairy, two-spirit,

bear, dyke, lipstick, tranny, boi with an i, ftm, mtf, boydyke,
half-dyke, bi-dyke, queerboi, ex-straight,

and that's just the beginning!

'Cause trans is lhamana,

and trans is hijra,

and trans is mah,

and trans is wahina,

and trans is...?

There may be as many as a million genders,
identities, and sexualities, just floating around,

searching for the right person to snatch them up,
put them on, and proudly parade around in their new skin,

unrestricted by layers and identity,
and limitations of culture, society, and social construction.

This new gender is a function of inner desire
and genuine understanding of self to be lived.

So go ahead, show us where the bathroom is.

SUNSET

He gave me drink,
            diamond-clear water taking my thirst,
                      when I had given up hope
of tasting sweetness again in the desert.
            The road was rough, curves sharp,
                      made my spirit into an ugly clay mass
that only beats when broken, and

            I've been broken,
                      chipping on all sides even when
                                        there is fire,
                      but the cool of his hands running
                                        on my back,
                      smoothing over my chest,
            holding me like the wings of a hundred
thousand humming birds,
                      gently singing while I float away in him
                                        towards the horizon.
            My heart was a chest
                      at the bottom of the ocean.
            Its flesh encased in time,
piling debris on for protection,
            even my keyhole was lost.

But he washed me
            and we never got clean,
                      but we did shine
            like the underbelly of a seashell
kissed by sunlight for the first time
            as he warmed me,
turned my insides back to butterflies,
            dancing in a festival of light
                      spilling over that horizon.

His lips breathed back
a slow stream of hope,
twisting through the blood and bone,
commanding that I move,
so my feet stumbled,
and my muscles ached
with the pain of underuse.

He brought me to an edge I'd been to,
but never peered over.
So when the sweet air touched my lips,
my eyes opened to the water
crashing into my stiff body
as I begged the breeze to push me deeper.

So if I get lost in you sweet boy, *if I get lost in you sweet boy,*
guide me with the grip of that gentle voice
that brought me to your lips,
light-show through Portland streetlamps
we found for cover when we stayed behind.

I'll make you a door frame
while we travel,
and our hands can build the walls
with these poems for shelter,
one torn-out notebook sheet at a time,
words for art work,
sonnets for ceiling, and
haikus, rengas, free verse for foundation,

so when we find each other again,
we can stand in the middle,
holding each other
as the sunlight peeks through,

tellin' a story of two boys
who knew each other before they even met,
all vagabond fingertips
and fishnet eyelids sayin'

Hey

Let's take this house and put it on a cloud,
Somewhere between Kansas and Nebraska, and
Slingshot stanzas through the windows, so
When the dotted line on our tour maps collide,
We can write this poem one more time,
Pray that we can press rewind,
Knowin' that today is just a someday soon, and

Maybe someday I'll love you.

Maybe someday I'll love you.

SUNRISE

I underestimated his cock.

Thought sex was just sex
just like the opposite sex,

just like silicone dicks on my lips,
but when he slid inside me,

I didn't forget I was once a woman,
like I thought I would.

We smelled of free
post-show refreshments from a double bill.

I fucked him hard
just to see how much I could handle,

but in and out the moments,
my thoughts turned political,

retraced identity politics during orgasms.
Never been with a man before,

so I tell him the truth:

>   *I've never been with a man before*
>
>   *never been with a man before*
>   *never been with a man before*

Never been with a man before.

Never sat on a dick on carpeted floors
in a stranger's apartment.

Shit, this feels good,
our bodies rocking together,

this feels good,
my hands on his muscular thighs,

this feels good,
the coarse chest hairs under my sweaty palms.

I put my arms around him
and breathed in the weight of him,

a scent foreign, yet satisfying,
like a secret I caught in the wind,

pocketing the inhale before my memory released it.
But that moment, just like the dust and debris

clinging to my hair in summer breeze,
I couldn't forget it.

How it felt to be wet with desire,
and fuck, straight-up fuck,

trying to forget we just met,
trying to forget this hole was mine,

trying to forget his male privilege.

When I asked him what he wanted,
he said, *sit on me*

and I sat,
and it hurt,

and in that time between
ow and *ooh*

the room stopped spinning,
and I got off him,

almost falling over in hot queer dirty sex fatigue,
and I took his curls in my hands,

and had him suck my cock
until I came.

NOT GIRLS LIKE YOU

I did love her.

To those who say she died barely breathing,
       pinched under my chest:
       you will never know this woman
       who had to leave
       because I could no longer
       look at her.

It was the mirror I hated,
       the look of a girl so scared
       that she became stone.
Couldn't chip if I wanted to.

When I started to love another,
       things got ugly.
I didn't want to see myself go.

Where was the one who used to run into the rain,
       savoring the summer sky on her tongue,
       open-mouthed to take the long way home?
I was alone even when I was with her.

All you could see was a blonde girl and a shadow
       a half step behind her
       like the second blade on a dull razor,
       scraping away at what was already bloody.

I gave her my body,
       unbound myself in the darkness,
       the weight of my flesh forcing me
       to sink deeper into the dorm room sheets,
       falling into a lost love without direction.

I can't believe I let her fuck me—
        I mean her—
        let her fuck her.

The night she began to leave me,
        dinner was silenced,
        the waiter carrying our conversation
        from dish to dish.

We almost finished our break up a week later,
        my body slumped in Maine,
        her hands loosely dangling
        the cell phone in Boston.

I drove in as soon as I could,
        didn't want this bad thing to end,
        saw her at the spot we first met,
        didn't even plan it.

Heard her say,

> *I like girls—but not—not girls like you,*
> *so Kit, don't ask me why I chased,*
> *locked you in place through skin,*
> *and sex, and the words that never meant*
> *to leave my lips. I'm sorry I started this.*
>
> *And I like girls, but I like girls,*
> *so pack your bags ok?*

She said,

>*Butches can take care of themselves, right?*
>*Open your own doors,*
>*walk yourselves home?*
>*Tuck yourselves into bed,*
>*make yourself a house*
>*out of cigarettes and forties?*

She ran into the rain that night,
>asked the sky to make a man out of her.

I never wrote about her after that.
Either of her.

They were dead to me while I
>found myself stubbled and hard.

But after all these years, I still wear her,
>bundle those collared shirts in my arms,
>breathe in the burden she carried
>into the night,
>wrap my chest tight
>and ask her to come back
>if she'll forgive me.

I fear that she'll never forgive me,
>that the mirror will crack if I ask her
>to come home.

QUEER HEARTACHE

It was almost Valentine's Day
        when I gave up on being queer.

I went to an singles speed dating event
        for straight people
in the back room of a midtown bar in New York City,
        greeted by sloppy chicken wings,
soggy egg rolls, and greasy mozzarella sticks
        to soak up the drinks.

And then the main event:
        they gave women metal locks
worn on a chain around their necks,
        and men keys!

Here's how it worked:
        I was supposed to go up to a woman,
say something charming, manly, and suave, like:
        Wassup baby,
I've been waiting my whole life to open you up!

And then put my key in her lock!
        I thought,
is this really how straight people date
        these days?

Then after all the white women had been approached
        by all the white men,
they last-resort talked to me:
        Do you wanna try your key in me?
        Try to unlock me—
        Hey, put your key in me!
                EW!

On Valentine's day,
          I tried it again,
a different venue,
          buffet dinner,
expensive drinks.
          Dressier.
          Stealth.

Here's what I know:
          I was out of place,
a fish in a willow flopping from branch to branch,
          searchin' for water.
What was I doing here?

Recently dumped, I thought maybe
          if I gave up on being queer,
intentional, feminist, political,
          I could find someone who would let me
be all the bullshit I fought so hard against.
          Straight speed dating:
that was my short-sighted solution.

          It was a bad idea,
because I came locked.

My body's been frozen,
          the deep kind that makes me brittle,
blood and bone and spirit memory,
          sayin' I don't belong,
there's a big queer sea,
          waiting for me to find my compass.

I took a lot of T the weeks around speed dating,
        been lyin' to the doctors
to get as much testosterone as I can,
        tell them I'm going on a long trip,
that I finished my vial,
        that I need more, always need more.

Regulated by state, expensive insurance,
        so I hoard it for times like these
to make the heart hard.

Mess with the doses,
        don't trust the doctors,
they don't know shit.

It's all talk about levels,
        the devil inside me,
a little more when I'm stressed,
        a little less trying to be less
like the men in my family,
        black-out anger, red-eyed crazy.
Desperation settin' me straight.

Something's broken,
        their systems failed me, and
here I am desperately trying to break free,
        telling myself that heartache is queer
and healing can be too.

So wrap me in a rainbow and let's make brunch.

Let's go to dim sum,
        read Larissa Lai and Amy Sueyoshi, listen to Ani,
let's fuck and fall into the ocean wounded with
        hands holdin' the blood in for each other,
the sharks close.

Let's do whatever it takes
        to take this heartache
and make us a home
        that's always unlocked.

Edwin's Poem

So me and my little brother Edwin,
      we've always got each other's backs.

Sometimes, I drive him to school,
      getting chips, taquitos, and slurpies for breakfast.

Sometimes we go to the beach
      when we we're supposed to be doing homework,

and sometimes we go out to eat,
      finish our meal at Zippy's with two desserts
                      every time we go.

My parents don't let me watch him every day,
      I don't know why.

He started getting my back when he was 5 and I was 20,
      with my baggy boy's clothes and fresh buzz,

and Edwin, he was all Yu-Gi-Oh
      and piano practice, and

when the piano teach asks my mom
      about how many kids she has,
            she says two boys and one girl.

When she says girl,
      she means me,

and Edwin starts to scream,
      No, Kit is a boy, Kit is a boy, KIT IS A BOY!

Then mom says *ok, ok,*
> *I have three sons.*

Since then she's almost never said *she* or *Laura,*
> no matter how long my hair got
> > or how tight my clothes fit.

But Edwin, he gets it so easily:
> I was his sister, and now I'm his trans brother.

We get each other at every stage.

When he was 6,
> I asked him if he had a boyfriend or a girlfriend,

He said, *BLEGH,*
> *I'm too small to have a boyfriend or a girlfriend!*

I said, *ok, ok, silly question.*
> A question that would have had my parents in a fit.

But Edwin, he gets it so easily,
> he is endless possibility.

He's 13 now and has a full schedule:
> baseball practice, media homework,
> > his first school dance,

and when we talk on the phone,
> I ask him if he knows that he should be nice to people,

no matter what they're wearing, or
> who they have crushes on, he says *yes,*

and even though he may watch GLEE,
      I just want to make sure he never acts like Karofsky did

in Season 1, bullying others and holding too much inside,
      hiding his fear in hate.

So, over the cell phone waves,
      I tell him the things that I wish I had known:

eh Edwin, you might not remember
      the things you do in school,

but you'll remember
      how the other kids made you feel,
            and that's how they will remember you too.

So because you can choose,
      choose to share your home lunch.

If you need to punch something,
      make it a bag.

Don't be afraid to make mistakes,
      knowing that sometimes you gotta say sorry,

and Edwin,
      if you want to try dancing with a boy,
            try it,

but if you want to try dancing with a boy
      but right now it's not safe
            or it's just a scene in your imagination,

then close your eyes,
        give him a spin. Press your chest against him
                and breathe.
      Because that's ok too.

The same goes if you want to wear mom's clothes to school,
      or a suit, or a costume,

they're all just costumes,
      so use them to make yourself feel beautiful.

I can see him on the other end,
      a little bored after a half-hour lecture,
           but nodding to agree.

See, Edwin's always been smarter than me,
      more generous, kind, and quick to share.

I wish I could be there
      to help him get ready for his first school dance,

but I can already see him
      having the time of his life,

in his new clean, crisp new shirt,
      dancing in a big circle
          with all the other little keiki,
            like fireworks.

JOSH AND DRAKE

When my little braddah was 6,
        he wanted a pet for Christmas.

At the top of the list:
        sheep,
        then monkey,
        alligator,
        sloth,
        lion,
        hippo.

What he got was at the bottom,
        but still on the list:
he got tortoises,
        the kind at the zoo
        the kind that outlive you,
        the kind you write into a will.
Edwin loves them.

So now we have two
        new members of the family:
        Josh and Drake.

And they love each other,
        I mean *really* love each other—
        they love each other so loud
        that I can't sleep while they love each other!

My mom actually once said,
        Kit come watch this cute thing that they do!
        You should record and enter it
        in an online video contest!
She doesn't understand how much they love each other.

And in case you don't either,
       let me paint this picture for you:
       Drake, the smaller one, is having lunch—
a bright red, juicy tomato—

and Josh is having *Drake* for lunch,
       right on top of him,
       huh, huh, huh,
       while he eats,
gettin' it on all tortoise-style for years!

That's when I told my mom that
       Josh and Drake were queers,
       tortoise lovers, boyfriends, fuck buddies, hot mates.
I mean I don't know their label,
       but I do know that they do the tortoise
       all day long, sleep in the same dogloo,
       and are really cute together.
I tell my ma that everything she raises is queer!

Which opened up this whole other convo—
       She said: *Kit, are you gonna have grandchildren?*
       Who are you gonna have babies with?
       Will you consider a man?
I need you to know, it's important to make family.

I get that ma, family has made everything in my life possible.
       I have plenty of family, all over the world,
       the ones she knows and the ones I've chosen.
And I told her that if I married a man,
       and had a baby with him
       we would be GAY and QUEER
and I would also still be with my then-girlfriend.

She gave that a serious thought,
        I mean a real serious mom thought,
        and said, *OK!*
On a ten minute drive to Grandma's house in Hawaii,
        I spit it all out: that I like men and people,
        I'm queer, poly, and I probably want to be pregnant.
And it went way better than I thought,
        because my mom just wants a grandbaby.

All this time while I was living on the mainland,
        Josh and Drake were having subversive conversations,
        engaging in queer tortoise activism,
        and blowing my family's minds
by openly fucking in our front yard!

Yes!

Ohana means family,
        and ours is changing, growing, and working it out.
So, thanks Josh and Drake,
        for doin' the tortoise:

        Huh.

CHOICE

On Mondays,
I inject.

Hand sanitizer,
alcohol pads,
thick syringe
pulling thick
testosterone
into the needle.

I replace the thick
needle with a thin one,
and flick, flick, flick
the air out the tip.
I stick the sucker
into my solid thigh muscle,
slowly press the sludge in.

I pull out,
rub the skin,
and let the blood dry.
I do not use a bandaid.
My body knows
there's no point.
It doesn't waste time
on bleeding anymore.

When I was a kid,
the needle slid in easy,
like a toothpick
in a soft marshmallow.
My flesh took delight
with the promise
of secondary sex.

Today,
the metal makes
my muscle twitch,
throws up the sharp tip,
leaves a stain
of oil on my sheets,
the fabric left translucent.

I know what I am doing.
I was not born this way.
I was born
both a blank slate,
and a million past lives,
and in my faith,
when I die, I will be
born again beautiful.

I recall, I reimagine,
I chant, I write poetry.
With this queer life
in my eternal memory,
I can only hope that this will be
a butterfly's dream,
flying, and fucking,
and dancing until tomorrow.

My voice a rehearsal
of every single moment
I have lived,
and pulled to the surface,
every breath stolen back.
It has taken me lifetimes
to choose, and my lifetimes
will be used to keep
this queer alive.

And when muscle
becomes cement,
I will jackhammer it in
as long as I choose.
I will do whatever it takes
to make this body feel whole,
build this shelter for a soul
I am slowly finding.

SHE

There was a time
> when I would freak if someone *she*'d me,
>> referred to me as a woman,
>>> called me a girl.

I hated the sound
> of the S attached to the -HE,
>> as if it were an assault,
>>> an attack on decades of gender journey.

My whole life
> killed in this three letter word,
>> S-H-E,
>>> She, she, she, she, she, she, she, SHE.

Today,
> the testosterone has set in,
>> changed my body,
>>> hardened my muscles,
>>>> hollowed my bones,
>>>>> changed my emotions,
>>>> made me feel and not feel,
>>> and go crazy.

When I think about the past,
> why I was so angry,
>> why I wanted to change:
>>> a part of me wanted to be in touch
>>>> with my masculinity.

I wanted to explore a side of myself
> society said I couldn't,
>> to be strong, confident, entitled, privileged,
>>> sure of my place in the world.

Another part of me wonders,
       how I've bought into the binary,
              the sexist foundation America is built on.
                     Did I not want to be a woman
                            because I wanted more power?

I ask this when I am given the check,
       as if only maleness is worthy of currency,

              I ask this when I am the only one addressed,
              as if a man's word is the only one
                     worthy of voice,

                   I ask this when I am given anything,
                     wondering if I have earned it.

Or did I not want to be a woman
       because I fear the feminine?

I ask this when I am called a faggot,
       I ask this when I buy makeup,
              nail polish,
                     dresses,

I ask this when I hear my given name Laura,
                  at the bank,
                    at the airport,
                       at the border.
I wonder if I have drawn myself a border,
       if I've stopped asking the right questions.

It's been 10 years,
        and I don't cringe at SHE anymore,
                on the phone,
                        or at the bar,
I remind myself
        that I am not ashamed
                of femininity,
                        of being a woman.

I remember all the strong,
        confident, smart, resilient women,
                in my life, and in herstory,
                        and to not put their struggle to shame,

I tell myself that this pronoun
                is not an attack,
                        but a nod
                          to the place
                              where gender is wide open.
I know now that in SHE
        there is nothing
                but power.

FAGGOTS

Sometimes in life, you need a family meeting.

For me, that came on a recent trip to my hometown in Hawaii,
watching tv with my mom, my uncle, my grandma,
and my little brother.

And as we sat there, prime-time before us,
I heard my uncle say to my little bro,

"Edwin, don't be a faggot...Stop acting gay!"

And this is way after I've had all my assertive, establishing,
experimental, borrowed, gay, lesbian, transgender,
trans, queer, b-o-i conversations with them.

So I called a family meeting, and by family meeting, I mean
freaking the fuck out while everyone was in the same room.

"Are you fucking serious?! Don't say faggot!
And don't call people gay!"

I ask my little brother if he knows that. He says,

"Uh, yeah."

Edwin knows that gay or faggot isn't a synonym
for stupid, dumb, or weak.

So now, by family meeting, I mean a fight.
He doesn't like that he's wrong.

My uncle says that I don't understand what it's like
on the baseball field: if you can't keep up
with the other boys, you're a faggot,
You won't get picked,
You're a loser.

I try, but I cannot change his mind that night.
No matter, Edwin is fine.

But it takes me a while to figure out why I'm not:
It lacked heart to heart,

so me and Edwin, we have a follow-up conversation
on the way to get pizza.

I say to him,

> "Eh Edwin, remember when we talked
> about using the word faggot?

He says,

> "Yep."

I say,

> "Ok—faggot is bad when you're trying to be mean,
> but faggot is fucking awesome
> when you're trying to do you.
> So if you are a faggot, you can say faggot, faggot,
> faggot, all you want, you can be proud
> of being a faggot.
>
> Because if you are a faggot,
> how it hurt in our family meeting
> last night will be nothing.

There might come a time
when you think you are the only one,
and if it helps you to think this, ok.
Because it's true, you are the only fucked-up,
beaten down, no-sunshine one of yourself,
and I am spinning out of control right next to you,
and a bunch of other faggots are too.

And before us there were faggots:
Auntie and uncle faggots,
big muscly faggots,
fat fabulous faggots,
sick tired faggots,
girl faggots,
boy faggots,
genderqueer faggots
funny looking faggots,
angry faggots,
nasty faggots,
sweet faggots,
angry-nasty-sweet faggots.

There is a whole library of faggety gay
faggotry faggotyness
ok?!"

He's like:

"O-K."

My brother is no longer on that baseball team.
My uncle came around
and pulled him out,
and I wonder if everything is OK.

I go back to my life as a faggot in a pride parade
with my tits out, and balding head.

I look for all the other beautiful ugly-ass faggots,
and I think of my little brother.

But I also think of all these faggots
burning together

in a deep sweeping gorgeous fire
that never dies.

Pussy Stitches

The year I turned 30,
     I decided to cut my own hair.

I told myself: that is a big boy move.
     So, after looking up the sexiest hairstyles
         for balding men,
     I decided to go with the buzz cut.
Its uniformity said to me strength,
     determination, and ease.

The fourth time I gave myself a buzz cut,
     I did a damn good job.
         I thought I looked like Vin Diesel,
     and a gum ball.

So after my haircut,
     I had a brilliant idea.
         I looked at the clippers
     and thought: PUBES.
These clipper blades are twice the size,
     so it will take me half the time!

After two seconds, all of the top part was off.
     Alright cool—now it's time for the butt hairs,
         and then I'll work my way to the lips.

After five seconds,
     I see blood.
         Ok, I have accidentally jammed
     my hair clippers into my pussy.
I tell myself,
     don't panic.
         It's not that bad.

So I take a mirror and I check,
        and not only am I mangled,
           but a chunk of me
        is now floating down the Hudson River!

At this point, I am still thinking
        about going back for the butt hairs.

But what I really need to decide is
        whether or not to go to the ER,
           and how am I going to walk in
        there and say: *My name is Kit Yan,*
          I have a pussy,
        I shaved it off with my hair clippers
and now I need stitches!

I'm trans*—
        I obsess over these things.
          At the doctor's office,
my body is a medical diagram.
        I decided that night
          that I would rather
        stick a wad of toilet paper
inside me and hope for the best
        than put my skeleton on trial.

I keep telling myself
        what I want to tell the doctors:

        This is my body,
      where beauty and ugly live together
like scars under binders,
        egos and demons dancing across chests.
          My flesh is a legacy,

and I can chose to crack these bones,
          cut this skin, poison these organs,
                    and still come out
                              a full moon.
I knew that bloody day
          that this was all I could hope for:

                    a love of my own body,
          a little more wisdom
to never take short cuts,
          and a hope to never need stitches
                    on my soft parts again,
          knowing that I am broken and bloody,
                              but whole.

Human Resources

They are giving out turkeys
                    at the Public Assistance office,
            wrapped in plastic,
                        legs folded in,
    balled for convenience.
                    You must have had
            to write your name
                    on a raffle ticket;
            I came too late
                    to see the process.

        There's something
                    about the Medicaid office
    that seems so familiar:
                    a waiting room,
immigrant kids sharing cheetos,
                        numbers being called in English,
            familiar languages
                    dancing in the damp air,
        chairs that are too big
                    and too small for us all,
    crammed into the tiny space,
                    spilling out into the hallway.
        The paper shuffling
                    almost sounds choreographed.

I reorganize my stack to the beat,
                    electricity bills with mismatched name,
application missing information,
                    naturalization paper
            with a little girl
                    awkwardly smiling, thinking
        they're taking my picture!

A notarized birth certificate from China,
authenticity always in question,
the tax return map
that brought me here,
to the basement
of this Brooklyn building.

It doesn't look like Fifth Avenue;
the designer fashion is knock off,
second hand
across generations.
The nails aren't manicured.

It doesn't look like Fifth Avenue,
but this is the backbone
of Fifth Avenue:
security,
deep fryer,
diner server,
window washer,
children of those
who breathed life into the soil,
before the buildings,
before the ships.

These are the brick layers laid off,
big families to keep warm.
These are the feet
that shuffle past the taxi cabs,
piling into the subway,
taking the day off
to come here,
to translate,
to apply,

re-apply,
and to wait.
For:

my body to be
an academic text,
my waiting line time a statistic,
my story boiled down
into a sound bite well-edited,
funders in line
to see what happens next.

I've been to Human Resources before,
my mother holding my hand,
the application stacks
for our family members,
the days I spent back and forth
social security to HRA.
This is not the first time—
just the first time my mother
doesn't know.

I've told her:
New York streets are paved with gold;
jobs and trees are fields for harvest.
I don't want her to worry about me.
I've got plenty here ma.

The man behind the desk is kind
while taking down my information,
the others that wait are patient,
lending pens and smiles,
paper shuffling some sort of comforting
shared experience,
saying: *You are alive.*

At night,
I am a single young Chinese man
ordering noodles
on a low-traffic Chinatown street.
It's the middle of the darkness
and this is what my last 2 bucks can buy.
A woman comes—
we don't speak the same dialect,
but she knows something
I've yet to discover.
She brings me
a free bowl of broth
to blanket the cold fall,
the water flavored
with marrow and bone,
sprinkled with green onion,
and I forget that I'm vegetarian
for a moment to thank her,
sipping the hot soup.

Speaking English

When I was 12,
my father went to the hospital
because he wasn't feeling well.

He had collapsed.
The hospital told him
that he just had some anxiety,
even though the only thing
he was worried about was
why he felt
like he was about to die.

See, the hospital doesn't care about you
if you don't speak English.
They don't have the time
to figure out what you're trying to say.

The next day,
he was lying in his room,
when suddenly
he started to convulse,
his body curling and uncurling,
foam coming out of his lips.

My neighbor's mom, a nurse,
ran over to help cut him
out of his shirt,
to prop him up,
to help him breathe.

When the ambulance arrived
it was too late.

He was brain dead.
We sat with him
in the hospital for a week
before pulling the plug.
I cried, and we buried him
with a pillow I had just sewn in home ec
trying to make him proud.

So I understand now
why my folks wanted me
to speak English,
why my mother made me
learn a language
she did not speak.

I feel guilty
for all the times
I complained
about filling out
government forms
for them.

My mom and I try
to talk now as adults,
We tell each other updates
in broken Chinglish.

I cannot express
much of what I want
to share—that *Mom,*
I just got my heart broken,
Mom, I am going on tour, Mom,
sometimes I'm so depressed
I cannot leave my bed.

Or *Mom, I do not understand
gender,* and she cannot
understand me.

None of this
translates to Chinglish:
joy, heartache,
success, depression.

We don't speak
the same language well enough.
We can only express love
in the timbre of our voices.
Our words trapped
in a colonial system,
making it impossible
to talk to my own parents!

I miss my dad
even though I don't
remember much of him.

I moved to Chinatown
just to feel closer
to his memory,
to eat the things he liked to eat:
peanut candy, Budweiser,
rice, and cabbage.

I moved to Chinatown
to honor my mother,
my family, the infinite
line before me,

to hear the music in the crowds,
to root this queer heart
in the sweet, the foul,
the sour stench of our streets,

because they let my father die
in the hospital,
because they killed him
long before
he reached the hopsital,
because they won't even let us
in the hospital

if we do not remind ourselves
of the strength in our own tongues,
of the resilience, the resistance,
in our own language.

Acknowledgements

It would take another book to acknowledge all the folks who have supported me in making this art. So thank you to my community, my friends, family, chosen family, collaborators, and all the people who have believed in me. I'm so grateful.

About the author

Kit Yan is an award-winning queer, transgender, Asian-American, Brooklyn-based slam poet from Hawaii. Kit's solo slam poetry show *Queer Heartache* recently won the Spirit of Fringe, Artists' Pick, and Audience Choice awards at the Chicago Fringe Festival.

Also From Trans-Genre Press

Seasonal Velocities by Ryka Aoki

Seasonal Velocities invites the reader on a fragile and furious journey along the highways and skyways of discovery, retribution, and resolve. Through her poetry, essays, stories, and performances, award-winning writer Ryka Aoki has consistently challenged, informed, and enthralled queer audiences across the United States.

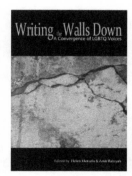

Writing the Walls Down: A Convergence of LGBTQ Voices edited by Helen Klonaris & Amir Rabiyah

Writing the Walls Down is a multi-genre gathering of US and international voices in an effort to generate a cross cultural and nuanced dialogue that not only examines the power of walls to divide, but walls as sites of resistance, (re)connection, and community.

Trans-Genre Press

is a division of the Trans-Genre project
an organization that seeks to support
and promote the many
creative talents within our
Transgender Community.

For more information on Trans-Genre Press,
Trans-Genre, and our wealth of inspiring artists,
please visit us online at Trans-Genre.net
or contact us directly at
Trans-Genre@live.com